ASIAN AND PACIFIC AMERICAN
TRANSCULTURAL STUDIES
Russell C. Leong
General Editor

    Bulletproof Buddhists and Other Essays
        Frank Chin

    A Ricepaper Airplane
        Gary Pak

    New Spiritual Homes: Religion and Asian Americans
        David Yoo, ed.

    Words Matter: Conversations with Asian American Writers
        King-Kok Cheung, ed.

    Music through the Dark: A Tale of Survival in Cambodia
        Bree Lafrenier

    Tomorrow's Memories: A Diary, 1924–1928
        Angeles Monrayo

    Fighting Tradition: A Marine's Journey to Justice
        Captain Bruce I. Yamashita, USMCR

    The 1.5 Generation: Becoming Korean American in Hawai'i
        Mary Yu Danico

Kathy J. Phillips
Photography by Joseph Singer

This Isn't a Picture I'm Holding
Kuan Yin

UNIVERSITY OF HAWAIʻI PRESS
HONOLULU

IN ASSOCIATION WITH

UCLA ASIAN AMERICAN STUDIES CENTER
LOS ANGELES

The author and the photographer would like to acknowledge the support, both material and spiritual, of the following helpers: Belle K. Bernatowicz, Arien Grabbe, Dr. Bion Griffin, Elizabeth Hare, Ruth Ellen Lindenberg, Reverend Irene Matsumoto, Dr. Loretta Petrie, Dr. Michael Saso, Hardy Spoehr, and John Sutherland. We would especially like to thank the Hawai'i Council for the Humanities for a generous publication grant.

© 2004 University of Hawai'i Press

All rights reserved

Printed in the United States of America

09 08 07 06 05 04   6 5 4 3 2 1

LIBRARY OF CONGRESS CATALOGING-IN-PUBLICATION DATA
Phillips, Kathy J.
  This isn't a picture I'm holding: Kuan Yin / Kathy J. Phillips and photographer Joseph Singer.
    p. cm. — (Intersections)
  ISBN 0-8248-2757-0
  1. Avalokiteśvara (Buddhist deity)—Poetry. 2. Buddhist poetry, American. 3. Hawaii—Poetry. I. Title II. Intersections (Honolulu, Hawaii).

PS3616.H456T48 2004
811'.6—dc22   2003063421

University of Hawai'i Press books are printed on acid-free paper and meet the guidelines for permanence and durability of the Council on Library Resources.

Contents

Introduction / 1

Wake / 21

Kuan Yin Is Mobbed by Reporters at Honolulu International Airport / 25

Valley of the Temples, Oʻahu / 27

Crack Seed / 28

Crush / 31

There Was Some Debate / 32

Kuan Yin Faces Charges / 34

Kuan Yin Mingles with the Ghosts, Now on Guided Tour, of the Slave Population Which Constructed the Great Wall of China / 36

Kuan Yin Turns Her Photo Album to a Certain Point / 38

Columbia Glacier / 41

The Grandmother / 42

Kuan Yin in the Folds of an Old Letter / 44

Kuan Yin at the Honolulu Academy of Arts / 47

After Thirty Years / 49

Lotus Hook / 53

Kuan Yin Rides to the Hunt / 55

Kuan Yin, Inventor / 56

Some Days / 59

Pent / 61

Tozen's White-Robed Kannon / 65

Ryozen's White-Robed Kannon / 66

Lin Ruyi's White-Robed Kuan Yin / 67

Narcissus on Chinese New Year
(OR: Kuan Yin Instructs the Student
How to Change the Face of the World) / 70

Problems in Taxonomy / 73

Kuan Yin Takes the Long View / 75

To Kuan Yin / 77

While Kuan Yin Waits at the Airport / 80

Kannon Submits to Freedom
in the Tea Ceremony / 83

This Isn't a Picture I'm Holding / 85

Jellyfish / 88

Cambodian Collage / 91

Happy Land Ltd. / 93

Kannon Sweeps Up at the
Moʻiliʻili Japanese Cemetery / 95

Stuck at the Buddha's First Precept / 97

Predictable Fire, 1911 / 99

Testimonial / 103

Kannon Goes Bon Dancing / 104

Statue of Kannon Brought
Back by a Soldier / 107

To Please a Buddha / 109

Kuan Yin as the One Who Sees Sounds / 112

Who Reads, Who Writes / 113

It's Natural / 115

Lesson in Ink / 119

To a Working Mom Whose
Babysitter Hasn't Shown Up / 121

Outpatient in Hawai'i Thinks of Snow / 125

On the Non-Duality
of Dung and Deep Waters
in a Brooklyn Museum / 127

World Wide Web / 131

The Named Is the Mother of
Ten Thousand Things / 133

Footnote to Vietnam War / 136

The Thirty-Three Sites of Kannon / 141

Mr. Alzheimer's / 144

Holding On to a Bodhisattva / 147

How Kuan Yin Loves / *149*

Kuan Yin Hears Cries / *150*

Buddha-Bodies / *153*

Photograph Sites / *155*

Acknowledgments / *157*

Introduction

You can catch glimpses of Kuan Yin all over Hawai'i. In Honolulu alone, she towers over gift oranges at the Kuan Yin Temple on Vineyard Boulevard and observes from her wooden and stone statues at Palolo Kwannon Temple as elderly women dance. She scans the commercial district in Waikīkī from a mural on Kūhiō Avenue, and she jams Thai and Vietnamese shops. She centers the crowds at the Chinese Cultural Plaza, hobnobs with waving cats on restaurant shelves (*maneki neko*), graces home altars, and rides the bus in laminated plastic swinging from a knapsack.

Kuan Yin in Religion

In Buddhism, Kuan Yin is a bodhisattva, or enlightened soul, who could "graduate" from the round of births and deaths but chooses to keep incarnating, to help others. The Chinese name *Kuan Yin* or *Guanyin* means "the one who perceives the sound of suffering," a rough translation of the Sanskrit name *Avalokitesvara*. Although Indian Buddhists depicted Avalokitesvara as male, his stories underwent a transformation as they passed into China. From the seventh to the ninth century, Chinese Buddhists may have combined the legends of the Indian compassionate bodhisattva with those of Tara, a Tantric female figure, or with stories of the Taoist Queen Mother of the West.[1] Her differently pronounced names include Goon Yum in Cantonese, Kannon in Japanese, Quan Im in Thai, and Quan Am in Vietnamese. With the exceptions of the male Kwanseum in Korea and Chenrezig in Tibet, Asia today predominantly represents Kuan Yin as a woman.

More than eighty canonical works in Buddhism mention Kuan Yin.[2] By the year 828 C.E., 744,000 statues of Kuan Yin had mushroomed across China,[3] and she remains one of the most popular religious figures there. In fact, after zealots destroyed many Buddhist artifacts during the Cultural Revolution in the 1960s and '70s, ordinary people undertook the finally permitted repairs by restoring Kuan Yin's statue even before the Buddha's in many areas.[4]

Rituals for Kuan Yin follow a common pattern. In home rituals, worshipers place a picture or statue of Kuan Yin over an altar and periodically light incense, say scripture, or offer fruit. At temples or outdoor shrines, visitors bow, light joss sticks, leave fruits and flowers, or burn paper money for ancestors. To ask for help with particular problems, visitors consult numbered divination poems by shaking a pot holding a hundred numbered sticks until one or two sticks fall out; they privately interpret the relevant passage in a Kuan Yin divination book or seek the advice of an intermediary.[5]

People pray to Kuan Yin about a wide range of topics, from the mundane to the philosophical, or from the self-serving to the community-minded, depending on whether the worshiper is asking, "What can she do for me?" or "What can I do to be more like her?" The *Lotus Sutra* credits Kuan Yin with the ability to intervene actively in catastrophes, stilling tempests or plucking victims from bandits. As part of Kuan Yin's association with Amitābha Buddha in Pure Land Buddhism, people may call on her to escort the soul after death to the Western Paradise.

A lovely passage in the *Lotus Sutra* explains how this bodhisattva can take any form:

> for living beings who are capable of being saved by a Buddha, the Bodhisattva Kuan-yin appears as a Buddha's body to teach the Dharma.... For those who are capable of being saved by the disciple, the Bodhisattva appears as a disciple to teach the Dharma.... For those who are capable of being saved by a woman, a housewife ... the Bodhisattva appears as a woman, housewife ... For those who are capable of being saved by a Naga [earth spirit], Gandharva [musician spirit], antigod, birdlike being, semihuman being, great serpent and others, the Bodhisattva appears as these.[6]

Because she can adopt many guises, Kuan Yin becomes not so much an external, exclusive savior, but rather anything or anyone who comforts or teaches another.

In addition to assuming these forms, Kuan Yin waits as inner potential: "by the practice of meditation the lake of the heart becomes pure and calm ... it is the reflection of a Bodhisattva which appears within it."[7]

Kuan Yin and Gender

Incarnating in a housewife as readily as in a Buddha, Kuan Yin contrasts not only with Western male gods and patriarchs but also with Avalokitesvara, the Indian bodhisattva whose stories evolved into Kuan Yin's. Ancient Indian Buddhism regarded women as inferior; one old monk gave the opinion that a bodhisattva would take female form only in earlier, less enlightened incarnations.[8] Chinese teachers, however, exhibited no such qualms about representing bodhisattvas as female.

Some of the iconography for Kuan Yin may derive from images of ancient goddesses. An oracle-bone text from the Shang dynasty, 1700–1100 B.C.E., contains the first written record of earlier goddesses, the Eastern and Western Mothers. The *Tao Te Ching*, from the fourth century B.C.E., also expresses reverence for a high goddess: "Nothing—the nameless / is the beginning; / While Heaven, the mother, / is the creatrix of all things. / All mysteries are Tao, and Heaven is their mother: / She is the gateway and the womb-door." Strikingly, this goddess manifests as a heavenly figure, not as the "passive, receptive earth mother penetrated by some sky father, as in so many ancient cultures."[9]

Kuan Yin's possible ancestry in a powerful deity who created the universe has led some scholars to speculate that the jar this bodhisattva is depicted as carrying may originally have been a uterine symbol.[10] Kuan Yin sometimes holds the jar almost upside down, with the opening at the bottom. In contrast to the male Yahweh of the Judeo-Christian tradition, fashioning the world all by himself, or the male Vishnu of Hinduism, blossoming out a new world from a lotus stem attached to his navel, a goddess would have gestated all life from her jarlike womb. The undulating lotus stem in some pictures of Kuan Yin could, then, be said to double for the creator-mother's umbilical cord, while her lotus flower would have represented, in ancient symbol systems, the female genitals.¹¹

While some scholars see the source of Avalokitesvara's transformation in ancient goddesses, others believe that, beginning in the tenth to twelfth century, representations of Kuan Yin as a woman compensated for the misogyny of contemporary Chinese religions, especially neo-Confucianism, but also organized Buddhism and Taoism. Chünfang Yü argues that "the Ch'an [Zen] rhetoric of nonduality and the Taoist elevation of the feminine principle ... did not translate into actual institutional support for women."¹² A female Kuan Yin at least allowed women an importance in legends, miracle stories, and art that they did not possess in the dominant ideologies.

Some of Kuan Yin's representations seem to empower women, but her stories at times have been marshaled to keep daughters and wives in line with current social restrictions. Worshipers have sometimes pushed the ideal of her compassion into a model of self-sacrifice enjoined especially on women. The legend of Princess Miao Shan, for example, which teaches feminine selflessness, was combined with Kuan Yin's tradition around 1100 C.E., when Miao Shan was called an earlier incarnation of this bodhisattva. The princess's father commands her to marry, but she refuses in order to withdraw from the world for meditation. When she fails to comply with his demands, he treats her harshly; in some versions, he even kills her.¹³ After the brutal king falls sick, an advisor tells him that he can be cured only if a person without anger donates an eye and an arm to a healing brew. Miao Shan, informed in her dungeon (or reincarnated after her murder), willingly gouges out both eyes and cuts off both arms for her ailing father. Variations of this legend are "performed, sung, painted, carved, recited and lived throughout China to this day."[14] Because her story glorifies self-sacrifice in women without requiring it of men, Miao Shan could be said to contribute to female subservience.

On the other hand, Miao Shan does defy her father's orders. She hopes for his spiritual advancement, but she works toward that end in a way that seriously flouts the Confucian morality of obedience, hence providing an alternative role model for women. And although Miao Shan escapes the usual domestic routine only by choosing a Buddhist convent, invalidism, or death, Chinese women have used Miao Shan/Kuan Yin to authorize other options. For instance, in Taiwan from the early nineteenth to the early twentieth century, worship of Kuan Yin contributed to a "marriage resistance movement" among women who neither married nor became nuns. These silk workers gained financial independence by forming sisterhoods and living in houses in which one room was dedicated to Kuan Yin.[15]

Instead of categorically stating that a given Kuan Yin story oppresses or liberates women, it is more accurate to see her lore as a space in which women may negotiate whatever social situation they inherit. While the women of the Taiwanese marriage resistance movement did keep to a traditional Buddhist belief that menstruation, sex, and birth "pollute" women,[16] the rebels still managed, through their devotion to Kuan Yin, to widen their choices beyond those of the traditional family. In a similar negotiation of power, Chinese "wu-women" or "soul-raisers" in Singapore go into trances to give much-coveted advice; by attributing the channeled messages to Kuan Yin, rather than speaking in their own voices, the women exercise more authority than they might otherwise obtain.[17]

In fact, the range of images, powers, and functions ascribed to Kuan Yin throughout her long history goes far beyond self-sacrifice. While the legend of Miao Shan puts emphasis on a young woman who passively effaces herself, other art pictures Kuan Yin as an old woman or sea goddess who actively rescues travelers. Instead of prizing virginity, as in Miao Shan's story, some lore describes Kuan Yin freely granting sex to anyone, if that role can lead to soul growth for her partners.[18] If Miao Shan's compassion pushes Kuan Yin toward an emotional side, a complementary image shows her as a thinker holding a sutra, as part of a tradition that personifies Prajñāpāramitā, or Perfection of Wisdom, as "a feminine deity."[19] From a variety of historical origins, Kuan Yin validates women all along a spectrum from sexually partnered to solitary, intellectual to compassionate.

The Kuan Yin tradition has been enlisted to upgrade the status of women in modern China through *The King of Masks*, directed by Wu Tian Ming.[20] In this 1996 film, set in Sichuan in the early twentieth century, an elderly man wishes to teach his skill in masked street performance to an inheritor. Because he has no surviving son, he decides to adopt—buy—a boy from a warehouse full of children sold by kidnappers or poverty-stricken family members. The king of masks initially is euphoric over his bright new "grandson," Doggie, but he soon discovers that Doggie is inferior goods: a girl. The master is so furious that he makes her call him "boss" instead of "grandpa," treats her as a servant, and refuses to bequeath her the art of magic masks.

Director Wu builds plot sequences around two art forms representing Kuan Yin—statues and performances—to relay to the old man, and perhaps to the modern film audience, a more egalitarian view of the sexes. The king of masks keeps a small Kuan Yin statue on the boat where he lives. One day the little girl demands, "What do boys have that I don't?" "Just a little teapot spout." "Does the goddess have a teapot spout?" "What goddess?" Fetching the statue, Doggie explodes, "Look, she's got breasts. Why do you worship her?" Here the film directly confronts "boss" with the contradiction in his religious and social beliefs; he looks troubled but makes no change in his behavior.

The film shows traditional performances about Kuan Yin that initially seem to perpetuate feminine subservience, but again the director teaches gender equality, this time through a growth of understanding in Master Liang, a male actor who plays Kuan Yin. In street processions, Liang impersonates the bodhisattva, as young women desperately try to touch her lotus throne to obtain the blessing of sons. Sons still provide women's one route to social validation, in which Kuan Yin seems to be complicit. We also see Liang playing a Sichuan opera version of Kuan Yin's Miao Shan legend. This theatrical Kuan Yin cuts a supporting rope and leaps to her death to help her father, an evil king. The performance inculcates in Doggie the old lesson of self-sacrifice, and she soon tries it out herself when the "king" in her life is falsely arrested for kidnapping. To get attention for her grandfather's plight, Doggie climbs onto the theater roof, imitating the scene in which Kuan Yin is precariously suspended from the rope.

Yet even as Doggie is preparing to copy sacrifice from the opera, the growth of the actor who plays Kuan Yin counters this example of feminine self-effacement. Liang's own social status has always been ambiguous; he is sought after like a rock star, cosseted in furs, and courted by generals, but simultaneously looked down on because of his association with women's roles. Realistically assessing his low position, Master Liang is used to reacting with modest if bitter deference; in fact, when Doggie first requests his help in releasing her grandfather from prison, Liang says he will ask an admiring general but quickly acquiesces when rebuffed. However, when Liang sees Doggie imitating him by cutting the rope, something in him changes. Still dressed as a woman for his stage role, he runs (in slow motion) to catch Doggie, then he forcefully reproaches the general. After grudgingly praising Liang's "courage and character," the general liberates the old man from jail, a result of the bold efforts of the film's two embodiments of Kuan Yin. In gratitude, the mask-king finally teaches Doggie his skills.

Although it may seem as if the master of masks softens his fury only *because* the girl has proved willing to destroy herself for hurtful men, director Wu undermines feminine subservience through the courage before power finally exhibited by Liang/Kuan Yin. He/she progresses from deference to protest; when he speaks out against injustice, he addresses both the street king's arrest and society's scorn against women or gender transgressors. The film ends by showing the quick-change feats performed by the old man and Doggie, initiated at last into the art of masks. The camera switches rapidly between the two artists, male and female, so that gender itself appears as just another artificial role, donned and doffed as societies dictate.

Kuan Yin in Art

As part of the gender shift from Avalokitesvara to Kuan Yin, some statues and paintings show a human form that could be either male or female. Japanese art insisted on a male bodhisattva for a longer time than did Chinese, sometimes depicting Kannon with an ostentatious mustache. In all countries, Kuan Yins of the last hundred years are usually clearly female. In 1997, to dedicate a new cemetery in Malaysia, a young woman of prom-queen qualifications wore a dazzling white gown and rode an elaborate lotus float to play out an ephemeral "Goddess of Mercy."[21]

Distinct art conventions have represented Kuan Yin for over fourteen hundred years. Either seated or standing, she is shown through a series of characteristic environments, identifying objects, and media. A familiar Kuan Yin rests with her right knee drawn up, right foot on the seat, and right arm extended over the knee. This posture, called "royal ease," conveys harmony of mind and body, both stillness and the strength to act. In a variation of the pose, Kuan Yin sits flat on the ground with her left leg folded flat, while she again draws up her right knee and drapes her right arm over it. In a further variation, she sits on a bench but bends her right leg so that her ankle rests on the opposite knee, both hands clasped on the ankle.

"Kuan Yin of the South Sea" also sits at ease, this time in

a grotto near waves. A young pilgrim boy, Sudhana, sometimes appears to the side, worshiping her on Mount Potalaka. Later pictures show both a boy and a girl, sometimes identified as Lung-nü, Dragon Princess.[22] In other paintings, the bodhisattva sits alone near a small pool, a bare foot pushed boldly into the water.

One of the most common of the seated art postures belongs to a type called "white-robed Kuan Yin," depicted in ink drawings or statues. These ceramic figures cram modern shops. Western Madonnas probably influenced the graceful drapery and modesty of this version, whose stark white is said to symbolize "the mind of enlightenment."[23] By contrast, earlier seated Kuan Yins in wood often bear the traces of polychrome, including bright reds and greens.

Standing Kuan Yins divide into several types. "Kuan Yin of the South Sea," in addition to sitting in a grotto, also stands on a lotus, on the back of a water dragon, or directly on the waves. A rarer "fish-basket Kuan Yin" appears as a rustic fisherwoman. One such painting, by Chao Mengfu (1254–1322), shows "a large plain woman with bags under her eyes, a strong common woman with character. Her appearance is extraordinary only because she has the long ear lobes symbolizing the perfect wisdom of the Buddha."[24] A standing, "child-giving Kuan Yin" holds a tilted jar with its arching stream connected to a sphere below her feet, where a small child floats as if in a uterus.

A "thousand-armed" standing Kuan Yin intervenes in the messy problems of the world. Sculpted or drawn with many implements in multiple hands, this bodhisattva usually looks male—though Siam Imports in Honolulu has a distinctly female thousand-armed Kuan Yin with well-defined breasts. In contrast to this staunch, aggressive figure, "Raigō Kuan Yin" bends forward deferentially, offering a single small lotus on which to carry a soul newly released from its earthly body to an afterlife with Amitābha Buddha in Pure Land.

Typical environments for Kuan Yin, besides sea, pool, or grotto, include a waterfall or full moon. Some viewers interpret the moon that surrounds her like a halo as a sign of "the empty and illusory nature of phenomena."[25] However, the moon could also be related to Buddhist scripture that says if a meditator can still "the lake of the heart," then Kuan Yin's image will appear.[26] Just as the one moon reflects in innumerable lakes and even in small puddles, the bodhisattvahood possible in all people pervades and potentially manifests in many different hearts, usually muddied by ego.

In artistic representations, Kuan Yin often holds a small jar or vase, one of her various identifying accoutrements. Perhaps originally a uterine symbol, the jar is later said to pour compassion or balm, the revivifying waters of life. Kuan Yin also commonly carries a willow branch, long associated with secular "feminine beauty"; the willow whisk as a religious symbol "brushes away evil of greed, attachments, ignorance."[27] In later works, the willow sprig shows up in the jar, though at one time they were separate symbols. Less frequently, Kuan Yin holds a jewel or lotus. A characteristic headdress or protuberance over her brow contains a tiny image of Amitābha Buddha. Usually this image is clearly defined, but sometimes artists leave the mound blank or draped, hinting at the indefinable Buddha-force that she reveres or projects from herself.

Although men probably wrote the canonical scriptures about Kuan Yin, women have contributed to her representations in art. In the late sixteenth century, Tu-ling Nei-shih modeled her Kuan Yin on a description of the bodhisattva in the Ming dynasty novel *Journey to the West*: "Dark hair piled smoothly in a coiled-dragon bun, / And elegant sashes lightly fluttering as phoenix quills."[28] Another woman from the Ming dynasty, Hsing Ts'u-ching, painted a series of Kuan Yins, adapting the conventions of Kuan Yin riding a dragon or watching the moon's reflection in the water. The Honolulu Academy of Arts exhibited a work by a Japanese woman, Tani Kankan (1770–99), who painted Kannon every day of the last four years of her life, perhaps a response to her own incurable illness. Did she hope that Kannon would heal her? Did she pray to imitate the equanimity of the bodhisattva, whether in health or in sickness? The exhibited ink drawing showed, in a few strong strokes, a dignified, seated Kannon in a simple white robe—and a dash of baubles at her throat.

In statues or paintings from any culture, Kuan Yin can most readily be identified by the characteristic draped elevation over her head, the lotus under her feet, a typical posture like "royal ease" with a knee drawn up, or a common object, such as the small jar.

Kuan Yin in Hawai'i

Kuan Yin touches many people who live in Hawai'i. While teaching a graduate course in literature at the University of Hawai'i, I asked if any of the students knew this bodhisattva. One local woman, raised in Japanese Buddhism, had grown up with Kannon. A master's candidate from Thailand reached under her very American T-shirt to pull out a pendant of Quan Im, always with her. A student who had left her homeland of Vietnam at age four with her father, an American-trained pilot during the Vietnam War, recalled that her mother gave her a picture of Quan Am at their last parting.

Kuan Yin came to Hawai'i with the first plantation workers. The Tong Wo Society Building, built in 1886 in Kohala, Big Island, contains a battered picture of Kuan Yin. In Waipahu, O'ahu, the Chinese Society Building, originally built in 1909 and now reconstructed as part of Hawai'i's Plantation Village, houses a Taoist and Buddhist shrine on the second floor. Mainly devoted to Guang Ti, god of war and wealth, the shrine contains a seated Kuan Yin near the women's alcove. Recognizable by the raised area over her head and the lotus seat, she is unusual in that she holds a sutra and looks quizzically out of a knowing, aged face. Although originally from a defunct temple on Fort Street, Kuan Yin appropriately occupies a space at the plantation, whose workers would have visited a watercolor print of her at the Kwan Dai Temple in Waipahu.[29] Moreover, each Chinese plantation worker would have kept a rice-paper print of Goon Yum (her Cantonese name) over a home altar. Such prints picture her alone, or with a boy and a girl as attendants, or as one of three Buddhas. Families continued to worship Goon Yum at home altars at least through the third generation.[30]

Today the main Chinese temple dedicated to Kuan Yin is on Vineyard Boulevard in Honolulu. A huge statue, holding a vase in one hand and a willow branch in the other, looms over a profusion of oranges, pomelos, purple orchid sprays, and incense. Yin Ling, a registered nurse in Hawai'i, told me about her experience at this temple. A native of mainland China, she explained that the Cultural Revolution had interrupted her high school education and postponed college. When the political frenzy exhausted itself, she managed to start university training, which she finished in Honolulu. But she failed the licensing test in her new country—not because she didn't know the answers about medical procedures, but because she didn't understand enough English. Reflecting that the Cultural Revolution had both halted foreign language study and necessitated that her mother's devotion to Goon Yum be expressed only in secret, Yin Ling went to the Vineyard Boulevard temple out of discouragement, curiosity, and a desire to connect with her past.

Under the bodhisattva's statue, she shook the divining sticks, and the number on the dislodged stick corresponded to the line "You've been trying to dig gold by hand from a mountain." Despite her hard work, Yin Ling was still unable to mine the gold of the nursing education she had mastered. Feeling known and encouraged, she renewed her "digging" with new tools. After further study in English, she retook the nursing test and passed.

The Tendai sect first brought the Japanese Kannon to Hawai'i. The gate to the Palolo Kwannon Temple opens next to a stone basin, inviting the visitor to slough off mean thoughts. A narrow, intensively cultivated garden dots red flowers among napkin-size leaves. The tall, granite Kannon, buxom and tree-trunk-thighed, stands outside grasping a thick lotus stem, and she shares with the birds the gruel put out for her every day. Inside the temple, Reverend Eshin (Irene) Matsumoto officiates. She says that her late husband, whom she succeeded as priest, claimed that bodhisattvas "transcend gender," although he himself used the pronoun "he" for Kannon, instead of saying "it," the Buddha-force. Reverend Matsumoto, in her warm, wry, and unassuming manner, quietly says "she."

At an evening ceremony in Palolo in honor of the bodhisattva, elderly women in kimonos dance with fans to the sound of chanting, bells, and metal mallets. Another ceremony commemorates the thirty-three sites of Kannon in Japan. Celebrants place their feet on a series of black-charactered, white packets of sand, collected from the Japanese sites and flanked by bright prints of the bodhisattva, specially unwrapped for the occasion. These paintings variously depict Kannon as female, male, and even horse-headed.

Also in Palolo stands the Korean Mu-Ryang-Sa, "Broken Ridge Buddhist Temple." Begun in 1980, the beautiful, brilliantly colored temple exceeded city height limitations, and the builders had to cut off the top of the main hall. The temple-keepers then renamed the temple "Broken Ridge" after a metaphor of the Buddha, who said that in the long line of his incarnations, a "house of illusion" had caught him:

> The ridge-pole that supports the rafters represents ignorance, the root cause of all passions. The shattering of the ridge-pole of ignorance by wisdom results in the demolition of illusion and the attainment of liberation or nirvana. As with the enlightenment of the Buddha, may the shattering of our own ridge-pole be seen as a purification of the temple.[31]

The main hall at Mu-Ryang-Sa contains three golden Buddhas; to the left of the central Shakyamuni sits Kwanseum Bosal (Kuan Yin Bodhisattva), represented as male. Outside this hall stands a gentle, stone Kwanseum holding a water jar and lotus. A nun who spoke to me through an interpreter called this Kwanseum "neither male nor female." The Vietnamese Thiền Viên Chân Không in 'Āina Haina honors a towering, white Quan Am in a narrow, vertical garden, her vase pouring from the top terrace, a red-berried tree crowding the middle steps, and carp powerfully darting in the pool below. Inside the temple is a memorial room with one wall covered by photographs of deceased loved ones, old and young. A shelf bears a few lit candles, while the opposite wall holds books and a row of varied Quan Ams. Especially prominent is a framed print of Quan Am standing on the back of a four-horned dragon, slicing through green-blue waves. This image comforted the boat people escaping from Vietnam during the continuing hardships after the American war. According to the Venerable Thich Thong Hai, these immigrants often credit Quan Am with their survival.

I first encountered Kuan Yin in Hawai'i in 1977. She teaches me a model of kindness and humor in an immediate community, as well as an ideal of activism against social injustice in a bigger community. My poems, which assume that Kuan Yin has lived through many incarnations, place her in the muck and muddle of everyday life, as do the photographs by Joseph Singer. While this book by no means represents all the Kuan Yins in Hawai'i, we try to suggest their range, vitality, and integration with ordinary people.

Whenever I have been privileged to read my Kuan Yin poems aloud at Bamboo Ridge gatherings in Hawai'i, listeners have responded with their own experiences of this bodhisattva. Once I recited a poem called "This Isn't a Picture I'm Holding," written after I saw a news article announcing the release from prison of a rapist who had cut off his victim's arms; a small photo beside the article pictured the woman at the courtroom. The poem imagines Kuan Yin as the amputated woman, then tries to insist, frantically, that the arms must surely continue outside the borders of the news photo. After the poetry reading, a young woman lingered to say that she grew up in a house whose altar held a statue of Kuan Yin—with detachable arms. Nobody would believe I had written the poem *before* hearing her comment. This odd mesh of memories linked us with the woman in the news article, with each other, and with Kuan Yin.

Notes

1. Diana Y. Paul, "Kuan-yin: Savior and Savioress in Chinese Pure Land Buddhism," in *The Book of the Goddess Past and Present*, ed. Carl Olson (New York: Crossroad, 1983), 174.
2. C. N. Tay, "Kuan-Yin: The Cult of Half Asia," *History of Religions* 16 (November 1976): 148.
3. Paul, "Kuan-yin," 174.
4. Martin Palmer, Jay Ramsay, and Man-Ho Kwok, *Kuan Yin: Myths and Prophecies of the Chinese Goddess of Compassion* (San Francisco: Harper Collins, 1995), 26.
5. Palmer, Ramsay, and Kwok, *Kuan Yin*, 98–101.

6. Quoted in Diana Y. Paul, *Women in Buddhism: Images of the Feminine in Mahayana Tradition* (Berkeley: Asian Humanities Press, 1979), 258–60.
7. Quoted in Edward Conze, ed. and trans., *Buddhist Scriptures* (New York: Penguin, 1959), 136.
8. Ibid., 31.
9. Palmer, Ramsay, and Kwok, *Kuan Yin*, 11–13.
10. Barbara G. Walker, *The Woman's Encyclopedia of Myths and Secrets* (San Francisco: Harper, 1983), 519.
11. Barbara E. Reed, "The Gender Symbolism of Kuan-yin Bodhisattva," in *Buddhism, Sexuality, and Gender*, ed. José Ignacio Cabezón (Albany, New York: State University of New York Press, 1992), 163.
12. Chün-fang Yü, *Kuan-yin: The Chinese Transformation of Avalokitesvara* (New York: Columbia University Press, 2001), 491.
13. P. Steven Sangren, "Female Gender in Chinese Religious Symbols: Kuan Yin, Ma Tsu, and the 'Eternal Mother,'" *Signs* 9 (Autumn 1983): 7.
14. Palmer, Ramsay, and Kwok, *Kuan Yin*, 78.
15. Reed, "Gender Symbolism," 169.
16. Sangren, "Female Gender," 12.
17. Mary Barnard, *The Mythmakers* (Athens, Ohio: Ohio University Press, 1966), 44.
18. Chün-fang Yü, "Guanyin," in *Latter Days of the Law: Images of Chinese Buddhism, 850–1850*, ed. Marsha Weidner (Lawrence, Kansas: Spencer Museum of Art, with University of Hawai'i Press, 1994), 167.
19. Ibid., 170, 176.
20. Wu Tian Ming, director, *The King of Masks* (starring Chu Yuk and Chao Yim Yin), presented by Shaw Brothers (HK) Ltd., distributed by Samuel Goldwyn Films, 1996.
21. "Cemetery Opens in Malaysia," *The Honolulu Advertiser* (24 November 1997): A2.
22. Yü, *Kuan-yin*, 389.
23. Yü, "Guanyin," 170, 173.
24. Reed, "Gender Symbolism," 168.

25. Yü, "Guanyin," 156.
26. Quoted in Conze, *Buddhist Scriptures*, 136.
27. Handout, Kuan Yin Temple, Honolulu; Reed, "Gender Symbolism," 163–64.
28. Reed, "Gender Symbolism," 162–63.
29. Douglas Dai Lunn Chong, *Ancestral Reflections: Hawaiʻi's Early Chinese of Waipahu* (Waipahu: Waipahu Tsoong Nyee Society, 1998), 245.
30. Douglas Chong, interview.
31. Abbot Dohyun Gwon, *Mu-Ryang-Sa, Korean Buddhist Temple*, pamphlet (Honolulu, 2000), 2.

Wake

Her one-hundred-
ninety-second incarnation
was spent
in the dark.
The sages
were stunned.
They could not understand
why she slipped to her darkroom
to soak paper
in trays.

Whereas they had watched moons
taking shape in their cups
(which they held
to the sky),
she waited out phases,
gestation of silver
in smooth baths.

The whales
breached the surface.
The bodhisattva
leaned from the bow
and aimed her tensed camera
(held sure
to her eye).
She captured,
that lifetime,

one-hundred-ninety-two
flukes,
disappearing.

No two flukes
of the humpbacks
are exactly
alike, flashing
as unmatched
as thumbprints of humans
(six billion, thrashing,
at this click of the shutter).

The posthumous,
one-woman show
of her works
hung a roomful of flukes,
like views
of one fan.

Kuan Yin Is Mobbed by Reporters at Honolulu International Airport

There was some difficulty in locating her.
She hadn't cabled a flight number.
Youths from the local hotels
held up placards for "Yin"
over muʻumuʻu, aloha shirts, and
$3.25 per hour smiles.
One or another would sing out,
"Kuan!"
as if from
sudden need.

Into air thickened
with frangipani and flashbulbs
Kuan Yin stepped from the skies.
"She's smaller than I thought."
"She's older than I thought."
"This orchid lei is going to clash with her costume."
"I hear she has eyes in her hands."
"Can't see her hands; she's carrying her suitcase."
"Why doesn't somebody offer to carry it for her?"
"Why don't *you* offer to carry it for her?"
"She was offered a contract to push hand lotions."
"She was offered a contract to sell eyeliner."
"I hear those eyes in her palms always weep."
"No good for mascara."
"No good for smooth hands."

At that moment of realization,
the first wikiwiki buses pulled up.
Since the welcoming party took up all the space,
Kuan Yin decided
to jog the concourse.

Before the crew had landed,
she saw on the green earth
the tiny shadow of their own plane
like a toy.

Valley of the Temples, Oʻahu

After driving past hills like pleats,
after swinging into the valley of the temples,
after emptying one's wallet at the turnstile,
after shooting the big log toward the big bell,
after fussing at a knotted shoelace on the threshold of the
   shrine,
after snapping photos of the big Buddha,
after looking at darting carp, like blue plates,
like flecks of gilt, peeling,
like a bag of orange and yellow and brown
floating M & M's,
after waiting in vain for the peacocks to show,
after driving to the beach,
after forgetting to lock the car
and finding the camera stolen, Kuan Yin
finds the Buddha
cannot be pictured,
leaving only footprints,
like nothing.

Crack Seed

The bodhisattva
knew with a shock
that a certain glass jar
(mislabeled "crack seed")
contained
human hearts.
Their owners had put them
(shriveled
and clinging
and soaking in brine)
out to bid.
Still darkly oozing,
the hearts vaguely remembered
their days of plum sweetness.
But mostly
they hugged the sharp shards
of the times
they'd been broken.

The bodhisattva
made a huge purchase.

Then she painstakingly picked
and showed the hard hearts
their still living center.

Crush

"I have a crush," confessed the student.
"Fine," said the bodhisattva.
"But I'm suffering," said the student.
"It's not uncommon," said the bodhisattva.
"I read that craving causes suffering," said the student.
"It's not impossible," said the bodhisattva.
"I could pretend maybe
 that my craving for the elephant driver
 is no more important than, say,
 a craving for chocolates,"
 said the student,
 placing one chocolate-covered cherry
 on a blue plate
 in front of her teacher.
 The bodhisattva
 popped the chocolate-covered cherry
 into her mouth
 and crushed it.

There Was Some Debate

The bodhisattva helped to open the egg
of the first condor
hatched in captivity.
There were only twenty-seven condors
left in the world.
The rest had been caught in high power lines
or picked off
as at fairs.
There was some debate
among the scientists in attendance
about zoos
or the wild.
The bodhisattva picked sticky shell
from her rubber gloves.

Kuan Yin Faces Charges

Here are the charges we have received to date:
she wears, if not miniskirts
of the most provocative sort, probably a
hair shirt. She seeks out suffering,
what's frayed in the design,
the motive behind the blessing
at the pasha's photo opportunity.
Moreover, we hear
that she flew to Niagara
not to ogle the falls on the arm of a beau,
but to flag our canal and flatten our house prices;
she sniffs out toxins
the way a pig noses truffles.
She's too negative.

We've heard for ourselves
how her heart bays an ambulance
like a hound on its chain.
When that wail's on a roll,
she wallows and calls as if those
careening dead
could catch the cadence.
We'd have that heart gladly
impounded.

Another count: her practice of pressing handprints
on objects she deems sacred
has left our city besmeared.
We cannot condone

her liftoff mark
on walls she's bounded over,
nor her ring of palm prints at heat ducts
whose breath embalms the homeless.

The corner musician's horn,
left unattended,
acquired a handhold in shadow gold.

But that odd buoyant dirge,
escaping down the alley,
soothes and sears beyond the elegant elegiac
which we allow.

Kuan Yin Mingles with the Ghosts, Now on Guided Tour, of the Slave Population Which Constructed the Great Wall of China

— I kept my self-respect by loving every stone I carried.
— I kept my self-respect by hating every stone I carried.
— You mean anybody who really wants to cross it can cross it?
— Well, it has aesthetic value.
— Yeah, it's like wrapping eleven Florida islands in six million square feet of pink plastic.
— Some would argue that aesthetic values keep out barbarity.
— Here's my old artwork: "Up yours!" I was blunt in those days. My bluntness has survived the centuries.
— You know, the airplane makes this wall a joke.
— This wall makes the airplane a joke!
— The wall still baffles the goats.
— The wall still baffles the ghosts.
— I never said anything at the time, but at night I could see Kuan Yin sitting on the wall: smiling, at ease.
— I never said anything at the time, but by day I could see Kuan Yin helping to lift stones.
— I kept working because I could hear Kuan Yin singing.
— I kept working because I could see Kuan Yin throwing stones down the mountainside. She was shouting the curses I couldn't shout.

— I gave birth under the wall. I prayed Kuan Yin to take the child before it grew bent picking stones.
— Did Kuan Yin take it?
— Yes.

Kuan Yin Turns Her Photo Album to a Certain Point

When pressed, Kuan Yin explains
why she has not yet left the world.
She shuffles to files,
turns to a certain point,
has to force a long look.

It is a famous photo.
Thousands saw the girl,
who'd torn burning clothes
from her napalmed body.
The thin naked girl.
The wide open mouth.
"Quan Am," she may have been screaming:
Kuan Yin in Vietnamese.

The girl would be twenty-five by now,
and then forty-seven,
and then sixty,
if she survived;
the photo doesn't say.

"She may still be looking for me.
She may not be able to forget.
She may ask me,
why?

I have unfinished business,"
says Kuan Yin, packing her sparse bag
with subtle salves.
"How is it that some are able to say,
'It is finished'?"

Columbia Glacier

The bodhisattva alighted
on the Columbia glacier:
like most glaciers,
centuries old,
ribbed and wrinkled,
as if its waves had been
arrested
on one day
of shock.
The bodhisattva meditated,
a bit cold—
lonely, said the press.
Helicopters hovered over her,
reflecting pinnacles of light by day,
training floodlights
by night.
The Columbia glacier,
suddenly leaping into the ocean,
would shrink up by half
in her lifetime.

The Grandmother

In her bunraku puppet theatre,
one small grandson,
sporty in black tights with black hood,
moved the feet of the puppet,
rolling them at the ankles like maracas.

One small daughter-in-law,
swathed in black tights with full hood,
moved the left arm of the puppet,
circling very fast like the outside racehorse.

Meanwhile, her son, dressed in dark tones
but wearing his own face,
moved the right hand,
the torso, the head.

Squelched in brocades, the grandmother fumed,
"Under my skirts are no
feet. I can't move; I can't
act. My very graces have been long ago
prescribed."

Behind his low bow, the son thought bitterly,
"My motions are hers.
I am effaced.
No one knows me."

And yet
there came a Kannon-moment
in the bunraku puppet theatre

when her three supporters
leaned as one
into the sigh of an old woman.

It takes years of apprenticeship
to touch the right hand.

Kuan Yin in the Folds of an Old Letter

The old woman
whose husband had died
went about folding the laundry
and said,
"I can
get by,"
as one of those
insects
(scrabbling
for memories)
for months
in a drawer of clean clothing,
subsisting on body oils
or the animal-smeared edge
of one envelope.

Guanyin Bodhisattva, Chinese, Northern Song dynasty, ca. 1025. Image provided by Honolulu Academy of Arts.

Kuan Yin at the Honolulu Academy of Arts

Purchase.
1927.

Kuan Yin is not worried
though she has a new background,
burnt umber.
It used to be white,
but she knows what it is
to be moved.
Still as she seems—
one knee drawn up,
one hand making the mudra,
circles, with breaks,
one arm stretched out
like the gutter spout draining
the woes of the world—
she has traveled
hundreds of miles,
jolted and bolted
in bleak boxcars.
(She knew then of others,
who'd be herded to trains
and transported to camps.)
Her muscles tightened
when the stevedores placed
their broad hands on that belly.
But everyone said
she sat the same on the auction block,
huge bids for the posture

dubbed "royal ease."
(Her hair trailing over
a shell-curled right ear
made her foresee
women's hair shaved and saved
from the ovens.)
Kuan Yin's sudden glimpse
made her rethink;
when her purchasers crated her,
sent her east to the isles
(she could hear from the hold
as the palm trees were clicking
like the sticks madly scrounging
at the bottom of bowls),
she seriously considered
just going on,
beyond the far shore,
or lending her polychrome
to the fish
in the sea.

She arrived
still intact.
But through subsequent rearrangements
in décor,
Kuan Yin sustained
damage.
Though a finger is held
permanently broken,
she has never been heard
to cry out.

After Thirty Years

The crazy at the bus stop—
grizzled beard, tan pants,
handsome, scuzzy, jazzed—
ranted at the kid on the bike.
The threat (the kid, the fit) skittered past fast.
The man on the skids appealed to the crowd,
"Kids *intimidate* me. Don't they
intimidate you?"
No one said they didn't
or they did. Meanwhile,
a faint rainbow huddled over the run-down dive
opposite the stop.
"Now that's what I like," Skids confided,
"a muted rainbow. I don't like a rainbow to be
too aggressive."

Once onboard, Skids held
his tan scarf to his veteran, frazzled face.
"Air trapped in a bus is so
bad," as if danger rode
with every breath,
the unexploded ordnance
from the unacknowledged bombing runs (a mission
every eight minutes, for nine years, in Laos),
the thirty million cluster-bomblets
still as good as new, the toys
boys left in the grass.

The kid called the dud a "bombie."
After thirty years of sitting,
it ripped through kidneys, patella, and part of a
pelvis.
The bodhisattva picks her way,
clearing mines, not breathing on BLU-26s,
trying to keep her rainbows
from glaring.

Lotus Hook

That white lotus in her left hand:
so light.
We'll let her carry
something soft,
something she can bear.

The emperor beckoned
his foot-bound wives.
As they tottered,
they displayed to raves
lotus hook foot.

At the opening of each petal
Kuan Yin can feel
the bone which breaks.
We'll let her have
something she can stand.

Kuan Yin Rides to the Hunt

Kuan Yin from her piebald pony
watched a falcon fold its speckled feathers
over a mailed fist.
The falconer, muffled in rabbit fur,
stroked the head of the bird,
warily,
and said to Kuan Yin:
"A falcon is a female hawk.
A tercel is a male.
A falcon is a better hunter than a tercel."
He unsnapped the leash from his lady,
who screamed across the sky.

Kuan Yin from her piebald pony
watched the falcon preening in the snow.
"What do you hunt?" Kuan Yin asked the falcon.
"Oh," said the falcon negligently, "rabbit,
 other birds." She tucked her head under a wing
 in a classic modest pose
 but was really digging a mite from her breast.
"Why do you always return to his hand?" asked Kuan Yin.
"Oh, because," said the falcon,
 nervous on the ground.
 Her dance left tracks in the snow
 with toes pointing backward and forward.

Eyeing the falcon from a distance,
 the falconers all said,
"What grace."

Kuan Yin, Inventor

Kuan Yin concocted
the first piece of paper
from mulberry and fishnet.
Her silkworms were chewing, chewing
mulberry leaves,
while Kuan Yin in red silk
was whisked to the emperor.
He deigned to unwrap
this twenty-eighth concubine
on nights of no moon:
not caring
whether she conceived
auspiciously.
Kuan Yin
tore off mulberry bark
and pounded a paste,
flavor: chewed wood.
Imperial gardeners
found her silkworms had languished.

Since Kuan Yin could not enter his presence at will,
the first sheet of paper,
apparently blank,
was presented to the emperor
by a eunuch.
The emperor bowed.
He did not know what to do
with the paper.

Now, at night in the museum,
after the guards
swing the iron gates,
Kuan Yin forages for paper
(empty cigarette packs, say,
smoothed open),
and with centuries-old ink,
found by the curators
slightly displaced,
she traces
a character for mulberry,
a character for fishnet,
through which she imagines
carp rising.

Some Days

Some days
Kuan Yin looks up at the bus stop
into the eyes of a 300-pound penguin:
bashful, soft,
and extinct. A jaunty feather
still sticks up on its head,
so hopeful it was
of courting affection.

Some days, walking on sand,
Kuan Yin feels the lurch
from long-buried torrents,
whose traces
even Sahara couldn't hide.
On those days, she hears
silent women walking, Plaza de Mayo,
bearing bloated photos:
missing children caught
smiling to cameras,
blown-up weddings.
There, in Argentina, soundless outtakes
are reeling, as, some evenings,
after a day's drive,
ribbons of road
keep threading her eyes.

Pent

When Liliʻuokalani
was locked in her
cupboard, her pew, her scrap
of paper in a pocket,
she paced
from escritoire
to window, wavy with
bayonets: bunched, ugly, blood-
seeking.

"Why," thought Liliʻu,
pent between
a new Christ on the wall
(pinned to his wood
by a blood-seeking god,
demanding payment for debt)
and ʻUlu in the stories
(cut up in a garden,
advised by his moʻo
to be buried in parts),
"why must I too
be dismembered?"

Meanwhile, Kuan Yin,
in Waipahu,
caught on a foot-square,
rice-paper print on the wall,
watched uncelebrated Sadie
bow, stretched between

parents needing money
in the old country
and a plantation owner
demanding payment
for debt.

Cooped in the cookhouse,
Sadie mumbled the story
of Miao Shan: Kuan Yin incarnate
as dutiful daughter,
cutting her arms, her eyes,
to brew a stew
and restore a mean father
to strutting health.
Sadie hoisted the noodle-pounder
for the umpteenth time,
smashed the dough,
cut strips.

Then one day
a later Lili'u and Sadie
scissored through the old stories.
They snipped out the lines
about sacrifice for its own sake,
to chastise the flesh
for blood-seeking gods,
demanding payment
for debt
(often by daughters,
though sometimes the powerful ones
liquidated lads too).
But Lili'u and Sadie let stand the lines

which said, if already hedged
and temporarily buried,
they'd will themselves
to be food:
the breadfruit, the stew, the wine.

Tozen's White-Robed Kannon

There's the same rock, angular over water.
There's the same waterfall, plumb past the moon.
(Or is that her aureole, her harvest
of perfect mind, bulging the sky bin?)
That waterfall's unswervable; her eyelids
don't flicker. Her robe flows as looped and white
as it did in fifty monastery sketches. Yet
what moved him,
what moved her
(after a century upright),
to lounge on her side,
to prop an elbow
on the water-worn rock
and lift her half-smiling
face to the falls?

Same sacred
protuberance on her head,
decorously draped with white shawl.
But given the tiniest tilt
of brush or globe,
Kannon could draw languorously to her feet,
stamp flamenco on her rock,
under red mantilla.

Ryozen's White-Robed Kannon

When old Ryozen in his monastery
sat down cross-legged
to paint Kannon,
cross-legged over a pool,
he knew his position
was precarious.

Stalling, he dipped his brush
into watery
soot, made from cindery
pine, and skidded a waterfall
tangential to the moon.
Kannon dipped her finger into her bowl,
nonchalant.

He knew his undertaking
permitted no erasures,
no changes
of mind or ink.
His task required
risk, dash, aplomb:
no regrets.
If Kannon's bare foot
happened to slip out of her robe,
she was prepared
to enter the waves.

Lin Ruyi's White-Robed Kuan Yin

Lin Ruyi's white-robed Kuan Yin,
Qing dynasty, is unexpectedly elderly.
Usually these artists
prefer a young bodhisattva,
slipping her leg from her skirts
to paddle a foot in the pond,
or they choose "Fish Basket Manifestation,"
when Kuan Yin "assumes the alluring guise
of an attractive maiden"
in order to peddle the Buddha teachings
to the young bucks of a fishing village.
Lin Ruyi, however, must have met
some incarnation of Aggie,
taking classes at the U in her 70s,
learning for the first time
that she too could pen papers
and size up the "greats":
"Those Greek gods and that Bible god
are both as mean as nails."
Aggie would call me either
"Professor" (no name) or else
"My love." She'd have a raft of young men
wanting to lend her books
or hear her angle on Faulkner's Ike.
In her white T-shirt,
emblazoned "Belt It Out,"
she'd sit knee to knee in my office,
explaining her epiphany at the movie house:

"Here is my Secret Garden" (pointing to the tiles)
"or here is my Secret Garden" (pointing to the louvers)
"or you're my Secret Garden" (leaning toward me) "or
 I'm my Secret Garden" (beaming).
 Parsimonious parsley and chickweed and dried-up pond
 though I'd been all day,
 Aggie could cull phlox, pluck carp,
 for her fish basket.

Narcissus on Chinese New Year
(OR: Kuan Yin Instructs the Student How to Change the Face of the World)

All you need
are a bulb and some stones.
Set your narcissus,
long alone in the cold,
where its crab claws can grab
pebbles and hug them.

Plan a mere
three, four weeks of priming
to dazzle the face of the new
year's day exactly,
flaunting pale petals,
sun center.

Plan, though,
ten thousand years
of runoff
to round
your few
stones.

Problems in Taxonomy

Baffled,
    they laughed,
        just because,
like some flaming
    flamingo, they said,
        some exotic
bird, Kuan Yin
    dunked her head
        into the saline marsh
at her feet,
    to feed
        upside down.
"Well, I like it,"
    she said, mildly,
        straining the brackish,
tide-tugged days
    through her lamellae—
        her whole body
a blush. "But ask her to name,"
    they said, indicating the gaps
        in their notebooks,
"what sweetness she finds
    in this feast
        of tears."

Kuan Yin Takes the Long View

Armero, Colombia, was a good town,
near a strong mountain.
The plains surrounding the town
were good.
A family could
not starve, could go out of the town
and plant corn, plant cotton,
which grew so eagerly
and puffed out so abundantly in the boll
that it was like the dream days of Quetzalcoatl,
when the cotton grew in indigo, in gold—
no need to dye—
to honor the god.

Did the Armerians recall,
carting their neat bales,
how their mountain blew up?—oh,
five generations ago,
laying low the village (one thousand bodies),
laying down the lime (millions of tons),
which, decomposing, were very good
for cotton and corn.

If Kuan Yin takes her distance—
the 5,000 miles, say,
from Krakatoa, Indonesia, to Hawai'i—
she can still hear the volcano
blow up.
The island just puffed out

like a kernel of popcorn.
If she takes the long view of Krakatoa—
from the stratosphere, say—
volcanic dust even there
can still
get in her eyes.
Krakatoa's dust blown to Hawai'i
diffracts more indigo, more gold,
into the sunset, simulating
the dream time.

By the way,
that mountain over Armero
blew up again.
It boiled its snows and slid mud
over the clean cotton, over Armero.
Kuan Yin took the long view.
But what, she asked,
was the view of the twelve-year-old
buried three days
in mud to her neck?
A camera caught
that cap of curls,
gold earrings, black eyes,
three days
to dream.
But only Kuan Yin could catch
a twelve-year-old heart,
halted,
in melted mountain.

To Kuan Yin

    Lady fish feeding
    Lady bread
    Lady waking of birds
    Lady who watches el Niño
        raging
    Lady hallowed horns
    Lady undoer of
        this my life
    Lady snowed-down on me
    Lady landfall
    Lady intellect
    Lady tectonic
        plate when it
        moved
    Lady joy of the follicle
        rupturing
        life, Lady
    Lady juggler
        who keeps innumerable gift oranges
        from ever
        falling
    Lady jukebox
    Lady blue Waiʻanaes
    Lady reacher of four hundred hot towels in an airplane
    Lady *pau hana*
    Lady history in a far land
    Lady swabbing
    Lady sharma thrush voice

Lady here
Lady whose image
    waits to appear
    on heart pond
    still tremulous with
    crash landings:
    water bugs.

While Kuan Yin Waits at the Airport

Under the stocking mask
instead of lashed eyes
stood the pools of a desert:
heat waves shimmering
the illusion of cool.
Instead of rough cheeks,
which his brother had kissed,
hung black curtains for Kaaba:
holy of holies empty of all
but what could be.
Around the outer edges of absence
surged his feverish thoughts,
like a crowd of exhausted pilgrims
limping their last lap at Mecca.

By miracle the stocking mask
didn't collapse on itself.
From under the edges coursed sweat
like tears at a wailing wall.

If a computed tomography scanner
had targeted that skull,
it would draw blips as on charts
beamed back from outer space.
Dead center on the ghostly graph
would loom two pointing fingers:
the fat swathed stumps
where his brother's legs
had been blown off by a car bomb.

At the airport, the young man
(face now stuffed in a pocket)
squeezed himself into a molded chair
on which a pay TV perched
at the end of his arm
like a prosthesis.

When he jumped to his call
(ready to blow that crowd
on an ultimate *hajj*),
he didn't hear Kuan Yin
shouting after him,
waving the paperback
that had slipped from his jacket.
Off sweaty blue plastic
she peeled poems:
ancient, linked
verses of forgiveness,
well thumbed, she saw,
but the book had belonged
to the brother.

Kannon Submits to Freedom in the Tea Ceremony

A twig
just juts
toward its calligraphic twin.
She kneels at her bowls,
the tips of her fingers
just touching the mat,
the earth,
the way the Buddha,
by touching the earth,
by calling his mother to witness,
routed fear.
She hears
water trickling
because she holds her ladle higher,
to savor the sound,
to appreciate everything
as if it were
never to be repeated.
Yet she unfolds her cloth,
splash of orange
tucked in an old obi,
in the same way
as always.
The first cup,
into which she pours
all her care,
her hopes,

can be tossed out
with a laugh.
She whips her unstrained green tea
with abandon
and sets the bamboo whisk
on its head.
Still kneeling,
she bows
with the tips of her fingers
to earth.
Here:
this is for you.

This Isn't a Picture I'm Holding

In this photograph we see
young woman with arms
cut off below the elbow.
It could be that woman
in the news.
In reality
somebody raped and hacked
her. In reality
it could be Kuan Yin
in this photo.
We don't see
any arms.
We don't see
very well.
Outside the photo
we can hear
that man with the axe,
giggling.
We don't see
Kuan Yin's arm and one foot
because she can step out
of this picture.
No.
She can't do that.
That man has stepped out
of prison.
Kuan Yin has no arms:
because the photographer

has cut them off?
The arms are still there,
I insist,
beyond the frame.
That man can pick them up
and lift their cold fingers
to giggling lips.

Jellyfish

Only Kannon
would know to love jellyfish.
They lay in the sand,
pulses of blue
in clear veins.
The jellyfish drove
never wanted to beach!
They strove to be
restrained,
but were driven
by squalls,
by tsunami
of love.
They liked to kiss surfers
at the crack where trunks
slipped. It was as if
jellyfish, though mute,
had been nagging, had clung;
when one guessed, it
collapsed, in chagrin,
and a man sloshed its mark
with his beer.
Mercifully, Kannon
drew, in her trades,
this abashed asker
to sea.

Cambodian Collage

Three red envelopes
for lucky money,
unstuffed, muffled thuds,
half buried in sand a
gold bracelet, not quite touching
its fleshless wrist,
just enough print
to set the viewer going
in the wrong direction,
enough pinned and frayed
burlap to let the reckoner know
just where the rice
spilled.
In one corner,
Khmer Rouge casualties up to
two million:
her explanations
won't stick,
stuck pigs have it better
than these cutouts, counterpointing

that solo silhouette of immigrant,
flipside
of the map.
He reaches for Lux and Tide
in the general store,
safe among the bulk beans and folk who are
normal (but superimposed on Saturdays:
humped hoods, wooden crosses,

burning half the page).
The checker's eye darts back to
other tides, bouts, boat
people, non-comic
pirates, squalls, swamping
sisters and all sense of
proportion. Here on the glued
linoleum, that fleck must be
Kuan Yin's slim water flask,
where it
broke open
its waters.

Happy Land Ltd.

Whether it's the Buddhist Happy Land,
where the good can grab
a celestial nymph,

or the vista of green cushions,
where the veteran of *jihad*
can squeeze his *houri*,

I've been shunted
to sex work
for a long time.

Whether it's the Korean comfort woman,
coerced to service the troops
of the Japanese Imperial Army,

or the *kijichon* prostitute in a G.I. town,
restricted to one day off per month
and fined half a month's pay for a second day,

I'd just like you brave soldiers
to have the courage
to look me in the face.

Whether it's a Bulgarian teen sold into Italy
or a Burmese girl indentured in Thailand
or a Filipina shipped off to Guam,

I'd just like to ask
you flush sex tourist
what you're so ashamed of,

why it's gotta be far
from any kitchen table
that knows you

and why you don't think
anybody'd want *you*
unless paid.

Kannon Sweeps Up at the Mo'ili'ili Japanese Cemetery

In taut, twanged sunlight,
she strolls the festooned lanes
(oranges, nibbled apple),
tips back the toppled tumbler,
tucks the sprig of orchid,
drapes the looped lei
of crown-flower over the cruet.
She traces the gouged characters,
smoothes the plastic photo,
pinches brown edges
from white chrysanthemum.
She breathes in
the incense,
serves *sake* to spirits,
pops open the Coors Light,
left for a buddy, and
forwards him his four or five
finger-size Baby Ruths.
Righting the vase of purple statice,
she runs her hand over
the rough-hewn,
defiant, phallic markers,
ready to lurch new life
in cryptic wombs,
with their own memory
of fire at the door.

On the way out,
Kannon ducks under
heliconia arabesques,
thick, rank, as if splashed
with red and green paint,
but she doesn't intrude
on the hermitage of green boughs—
tattered canvas doorways
all over, all shut—
where the hobo shelters,
as dismissed as the dead,
or more so, his abode
heralded by one faded *koi*,
flapping in permanent boy's day,
and, perched on the same branch,
higher than it's ever been before,
a deer: dappled, plastered,
kneeling.

Stuck at the Buddha's First Precept

    I remembered the first rule,
    to refrain
    from taking life,
    too late.
        It was late
        when the rats ate,
        chiseled their chunks
        of avocado, buttery smooth,
        leaving on the sidewalk
        sculpted, greenish-yellow
        splashes of excess everywhere,
        on the leathery half-shell,
        then, gamboled on to the next pupu:
        pierced mango, sucked on, chucked.

Drunk on luck, the rats
lugged back their loot,
caromed perfectly round avocado pits
toward one another in the attic,
skittered, squealed, chattered,
beat out delight
        right overhead.
        It's four a.m.,
        I muttered,
        indignant,
        and don't they harbor
        some sort of disease?

So old Mr. Buju,
landlord to
an unruly tenant,
hauled over the ladder,
laid out the pellet trays,
lids peeled back
invitingly.
    It was later—
    how long do these things take?—
    when, my key in the lock, my eyes
    turned and met the eyes
    of a small, slowed, unrollicking
    rat under the always-bearing,
    blue-flowered bush.
    Its eyes, my eyes: brown.
    Its eyes, my eyes
    blinked.

Old Mr. Buju,
small, bowed—
and sad? or is that
my eyeing?—
plodded away,
holding by the tail
dead rat, swinging.

Predictable Fire, 1911

    where was Kuan Yin (stitching),
    where was Kuan Yin (snipping),
    when the boss (on the bias)
    locked the doors
    at the Triangle Shirtwaist Company
    (bobbin, bobbin), locked the doors
    against malingerers (cut)
    at the Triangle Shirtwaist Company, where
    was Kuan Yin immigrant
    when the fire chief admitted
    (in the pocket, Triangle Shirtwaist),
    admitted that his ladders
    (on the bias) couldn't reach
    past the seventh floor (stretching),
    where was Kuan Yin (treadling,
    like rocking
    a cradle)
    when the boss, knowing,
    rented the eighth floor,
    the ninth floor,
    the tenth,
    where was Kuan Yin (rocking
    a cradle, inching
    away) at the Triangle trap,
    where was the baby
    (inching closer
    to the stairwell),
    where was Kuan Yin (putting in darts)

when the rags flamed (paper patterns),
where when the dailies
(snipping, twelve hours, on the bias)
reported "thud after thud"
on the pavements below
the high Triangle Company,
increasing their circulation,
where was Kuan Yin
(standing on a ledge,
increasing her circulation),
where was Kuan Yin (hugging
the next girl)
to leap at least
in the company
of Kuan Yins

Testimonial

On the way to Vegas, car went
ka-pow!
I thought I was
dead already.
But I came out,
nothing scratch.
That's Kannon.
Took five hundred dollars
home from Vegas.
What'd I tell you?
That's Kannon.
'Course, I left
four, five hundred
with one-arm bandit.
My wife tells that;
puts the damper.
But then, all told,
we had a ball.
Yeah. One blast.

Kannon Goes Bon Dancing

The old woman goes round:
white hair in a bun,
black-splashed kimono,
pink obi.
"Come try!"
The bon dancing club goes round:
aqua jackets, shorts,
checkered headbands, fans.
"Come try!"
Serious teenage boy goes round:
sheathing kimono, white socks, *geta*,
pelvis dipping gracefully,
taut dignity of the erotic.
The stars go round.

"Come try!"
Dapper elder in creased slacks
goes round in a blue-ferned shirt
and peppermint sweatband
and beckons Mercedes
to join the line.
"Come try!"
Laughing men go round:
forward, back, slide,
push. A footwork expert
goes round, omitting hand gestures,
the better to balance
his tiny son on his shoulders.

A line snakes round
to belt the drum.

The elder in creased slacks
draws laughing Mercedes into the line.
The stars go round.
Nine wheelchairs go round,
steered by teens:
forward, back, spinning in place.
Toddlers bobbing
go round underfoot.
The line snakes round
to belt the drum.
The rain goes round.
Pink obi is splashed.
Plastic rain hats unpleat,
fold back into pockets.

Mercedes goes round,
laughing. Her welcomer in blue
sits out one round.
"My friend taught me
bon dancing," he confides;
"before, only ballroom.
But she died,
January.
I learned,
have to be nice,
now." He'd coaxed Mercedes
into the line.
"Come try!"

Statue of Kannon Brought Back by a Soldier

I'm donating this statue
to the temple.
I got her in the war.
Well, you know how things were.
She looks
sort of grubby
(she did then too)
but she's got
a perky face.
It made her seem
like she still had flesh on her bones,
still alive.
She could thrive in a cave.
See, her arm over her knee,
so offhand,
made her look
not afraid,
and that one knee drawn up—
a toughie,
I thought.
Well, I took her in the war.
You know how things were.
She was there
so I just grabbed
this little
piece.

I thought—she'd protect
me; you'd
have to say
she did that,
right?

To Please a Buddha

According to the *Lotus Sutra*,
to please a Buddha,
place "bowls and bins,"
"banners" and "playthings."
Dip into the bins,
garbanzos and pintos,
pied red, whose polish
in a bowl to rinse them
rivals the stream's
caress over play-stones
it knows it must leave.
To please a Buddha, leave,
hurry on, pick up your
banner, hand-painted, pied red,
reading, "Make Methanol, Not War,"
as the expensive machine
bulldozes boys in the Gulf
over oil,
and the tiger-claw blossoms
drop underfoot
at the protest march.
To please a Buddha,
bob your banner and smile:
smile at the red claw,
smile at the FBI boys,
in telltale tie, brush-cut,
who studiously snap photos
for their files (their fantasies

played out), capturing an aureole—
"Make Love, Not War"—
from an earlier protest,
in blurry images
of somebody, or somebody else, whose
playthings are dragonflies,
mating in air,
she dipping down,
dappling the puddle,
as she drops her eggs,
he flying fast, her
pleased banner.

Kuan Yin as the One Who Sees Sounds

She sees a yellow earth-
mover, backing and beeping,
warning walkers now inured
to its bleat and to danger
as to the beat of a clock,
while the earth-moving pulse
spurts to Sarah, not sleeping,
in the old people's home.
In the next room
Cary confides to her grandson,
for the fourth time,
how she has kept her mind fresh:
"I've memorized all the Presidents."
When she gets to "Ulysses S.,"
Hugh in the rec. room
aims his billiard cue
and announces to no one,
"I bagged two wildebeests."
As Kuan Yin pockets an ivory ball,
she hears, among the quick clicking
and the slow winding down,
both Hugh's unsung wanderings
and the sound that a tusk makes
when it's sawed by a poacher
from a face which,
just a moment before,
was moving the earth.

Who Reads, Who Writes

Just so you'll know
I'm here (no,
just so you'll know
I'm not here),
I'll tell you a little story.
A brash young man from the zendo
calls up: "Have any more poems?
One for Blind Donkey?"
Oh, okay, fodder
for his newsletter.
So over he comes
with an older meditator,
black robes flapping on lanky limbs,
cocky as those crows in Japan
which deign to let the cars
crack their nuts for them,
dropping them not just anywhere
on the highway,
but cleverly in the crosswalk,
so the crows can saunter safe,
retrieve their cracked loot.
So, like crows
(no, what am I saying;
I'm here,
in Hawai'i), like mynahs,
all elbows and strut,
in come the zendo brothers.
Sam, the young one,

folds himself into the angular arms
of my broken-down chair
and leafs through the sheaf I hand him.
"Hey, listen to this,"
he chortles to Ben
and takes off into
"Kuan Yin Turns Her Photo Album,"
as sure of his winging it
as if he'd mapped the miles himself.
When he gets to the napalmed village—
"The thin naked girl,
the wide open mouth"—
Ben, quiet on a kitchen stool,
opens *his* mouth
and stretches out *his* arms,
same angle as the girl
in the famous photo,
reached back to him
from Vietnam War days.
Ben's arms
are the poem.
Sam is the poet. Ben
is that girl. Kuan Yin—
she took our breath
to speak. She took our breath
away.

It's Natural

Kuan Yin can draw back
all the monarch butterflies in the hemisphere
to winter on an out-of-the-way hill
in Mexico.
It's possible.
Some places are real.

It's clear:
the monarchs must be bearing
little magnetic bands on their bodies.
Well, somehow
they respond.

It's true:
they do have to fly over
the pulling heavy metals
dumped into the Río Nuevo,
distended dead dogs.

The orange and black butterflies
are waiting
on a milkweed patch in Kentucky.
That river is an outbreak
waiting to happen.

As Kuan Yin climbs the high paths,
thousands of the long-distance experts
teeter on her forearm,
cling to her robe.

They importune her eyelids
and dash against the transmitter
strapped to her ankle,
not knowing
they're home.

Raigō Kannon, Japanese, Kamakura Period (1185–1393).
Image provided by Honolulu Academy of Arts.

Lesson in Ink

Here, said the student,
handing Kuan Yin a crumpled scroll,
is my life. I'm renouncing
the world.
The student had managed to knot
the still untied tassel,
but Kuan Yin loosed it and said:

You must live your life like a
hand scroll, you only get a glimpse at
a go; meaning is a monkey's
foot, gone by the time of
tail, and the next monkey,
peeping, doesn't care about
plans, doesn't know whether
pains inflicted on her
by powers that be
yielded test results
that ever saved
a life or two, other than
her own. Instead of total
picture she's linked only to one,
wait, two other monkeys, who
are inspecting something, a
crab, the way you can
inspect your scroll with me,
though usually all by your-
self, yet maybe one other
over your shoulder

who just appears,
like this brief poem of three,
no, four columns and don't complain to
me if your wrist gets cramped
because you want so much to open
this scroll continuously.

To a Working Mom Whose Babysitter Hasn't Shown Up

No, it doesn't say in the Sutras
(I checked) what to do
when the babysitter hasn't shown up
and it's time to conduct the mentoring meeting
at the office
and the six-year-old is dragging along a grudge
left over from school.

No, it doesn't say in the Verses
(I'm hunting) how to proceed
after you've set the six-year-old to drawing
rhinos at the blackboard
and he keeps screeching through the meeting,
"Hey, Mom, look,"
and details your failings aloud to the rhinos.

No, it doesn't say in the Glosses
(I've consulted them) how to respond
after you've suggested he might munch
the Mars Bar in your purse
and he dumps everything out
in the middle of the mentees:
rubber-bands tampon checkbook car-keys.

No, it doesn't say in the Birth-Stories
(I'm looking) how to get through
this particular incarnation,
as you're hurrying your son down the street
to pick up his sister at daycare

and, three-year-old on hip, books on back,
her sack on arm, him in tow,
you can't find the car-keys.

No, it doesn't say in the Expositions
(I'm flipping through as fast as I can) how to get back
into the office,
or whether the security guard really has
a legitimate reason
for not leaving his station,
or whether it might not be a better idea
just to head for the bus stop.

No, it doesn't say in the Similes
(I tried) how to feel
after you've perched the three-year-old, the book bag,
the sack, yourself, on the edge of the fountain in the plaza,
and the six-year-old announces nonchalantly,
"There go her slippers,"
and you look up to see hot-pink footwear
floating away.

But, wait, it might say here in the Marvels
after you've jumped into the fountain in your shoes,
and cool water is lapping your thighs,
and the sun's going down,
and the mynahs are exulting in the monkey pod tree,
and you suddenly start laughing,
yes, it says right here, it's Kannon
who puts her foot in the pool.

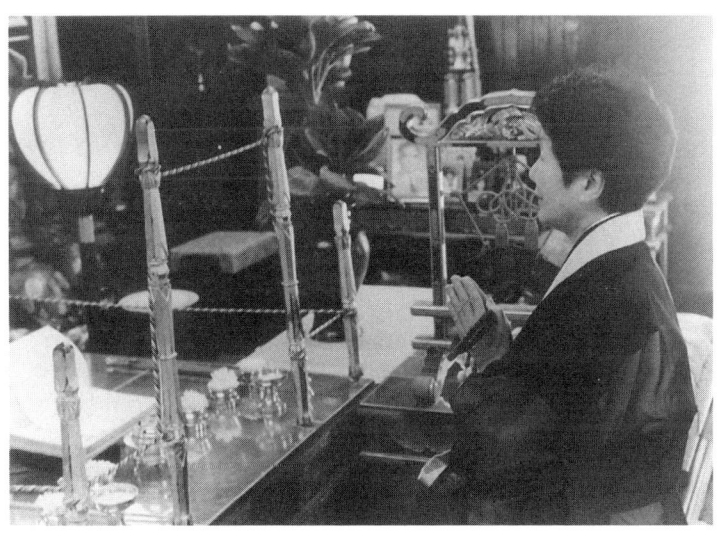

Outpatient in Hawai'i Thinks of Snow

During the four-hour drip,
like icicles off a roof,
the Rituxin slips into veins
to melt cells spelling
lymphoma,
lymphoma, on a jag.
Meanwhile, the patient,
pinned down as landscape,
thinks, I could be elsewhere,
be Kuan Yin, turning her hand
to microphotography, say, catching
snow crystals, with Bentley and the best
of the old scientists, those
attenders to small wonders.
You just reach your slate to the falling
sky, then dash into the freezing
shed, to transfer the stash to a
glass, stroking your private cache
of snow
with a feather.
Then: hold contraption to light!
Wait: could all this loveliness
really be colorless nothing?
Who cares? Uncover the lens
for all your twenty seconds!
And would you look at these snaps?
Whether plunked down in the Andes or the Alps,
Minnesota or the top of Mauna Kea,

the pattern is pretty much the same:
a six-sided spurt of birth
to death and back,
some squiggles in between,
tiresome, really, but what surprising knobs
and nubs!
nibs and bulbs!
blobs and blips,
dips and doodles,
doodads, darnings,
ouch, darn this drip;
I guess, doc, I don't need
to inspect *all* the flakes
to catch the drift,
but, still, to make *sure*
they're each unique,
I'd better
turn over
every
last
one.

On the Non-Duality of Dung and Deep Waters in a Brooklyn Museum

> *Release this elephant which is your mind,*
> *that he may drink the river-waters*
> *and stay on the bank at his pleasure.*
> —Saraha, "Treasury of Songs,"
> ninth century C.E.

Right there in Brooklyn,
the artist mosaicked
a radiant Mother Maria,
DAUBED WITH ELEPHANT DUNG.

Mother Maria sauntered through
her dusty village,
through naked toddlers,
her broad bare feet—
DAUBED WITH ELEPHANT DUNG—

cracked like a riverbed
where the elephants know
they have to go further to siphon up water
to hose down (trunk down)
their dusty backs.

Back in the city,
the mayor objected
that Mother Maria
in a blue smock
and a black skin

was planting her broad foot
in a dusty road
DAUBED WITH ELEPHANT DUNG.

The mayor impounded
the museum's subsidy,
seven million dollars,
because he wanted,
said the press release
DAUBED WITH ELEPHANT DUNG,
to give—oh, a hundred
of those Art-Wasted dollars
to spruce up Mother Maria's village
and buy it a new water pump,
named for the mayor.

But the mayor hadn't checked
if the water table might hold
traces of naturally occurring arsenic
that would poison the villagers,
never before exposed
to such DEEP WATERS.

With the rest of the millions,
the mayor purchased
innumerable blue and yellow plastic buckets
for a radiant brigade of Brooklynites
to slosh down
the offending painting
DAUBED WITH ELEPHANT DUNG.

Reading in the newspaper
about the mayor's magnanimous plans,

an old man in dusty Brooklyn
got off the El
at an underground station
DAUBED WITH ELEPHANT
(and other cosmopolitan) DUNG

and trudged up the urine-sprayed steps,
all the while vigorously shaking his can of white paint
and listening to the satisfying staccato
of a metal ball batting madly against the metal insides

and mixing every last drop
of linseed oil and lead and
whatever else was still in the stuff
but sure to be phased out
in the near future
DAUBED WITH ELEPHANT DUNG.

The old man forked over
his entrance fee to the museum, wandered around,
lingered at the lone Kuan Yin statue,
foot drawn up on her bench, most unladylike,
and finally ferreted out,
with some difficulty, Mother Maria,
lost in the crowd come to inspect
a satisfying scandal
DAUBED WITH ELEPHANT DUNG.

Then the dusty old man
slipped his weapon from his trench coat
and siphoned up his Lily White,
on Special,

intending to re-virginize
Mother Maria,

but instead, as he hosed down
(aerosoled down)
her portrait, she turned again the finely cracked white
of old ELEPHANT DUNG,
calcified and radiant, in village sun.

World Wide Web

I hear Kuan Yin
has her own website
or sites, a world of
dots and double
yous; I'm trying to see
who *you* might
be, a channeler, maybe,
for "Lady Kuan Yin herself" to
"update you on my activities
at this point
in your time frame."
In my frame I scroll down, annoyed,
and this channeled Kuan Yin
starts to scold
me, but if I scold
you for scolding, am I
not still *you*? Oh.
And if I can't get out of that
mind frame, at the end of this life it's
BACK TO MENU.
But then, what the heck:
"I AM FOOD,"
says the playful Self of the *Upanishads*,
and if you chew me up, you'll
still be me and I,
you, or something like that:
@ ! @ ! @ ! @ ! @ ! @ !
So *Klicken Sie hier* and see

a new site, where
"Etherically, Lady Kuan Yin has
preceded Saint Germain
as Chohan of the Seventh Ray"
and "serves as the
representative of the Seventh Ray
on the Karmic Board,"
a cross between Byzantium
and Wall Street,
and, sure enough, there she is, a merchant:
"Kuan Yin Goddess (pair) $19.98."
Kuan Yin, you're a card, a pair, a crowd,
dew dots stuck in
Indra's web, where
each of our faces
picks up
each of our faces.

The Named Is the Mother of
Ten Thousand Things

This was back in college
in a college town
on a snowy night
when my suite mate and I
(she from Taiwan, I from New Jersey)
strolled by the bookstore,
ducked in to warm up.
We stood by the *Tao Te Ching*,
dual-language edition,
with black-and-white photos
(a wide, welcoming book)
and read, side by side,
the Chinese on the left
or the English on the right,
while a photo of sparse pine
shadowed the inked tree of characters
and a photo of birch bark
backed the striped script,
until every now and then
this beckoning book
called the calligraphy to the right
and led the letters to the left,
so we (the two readers)
would silently switch places,
as the snow melted from our woolen coats

and my glasses steamed up,
just as Avalokitesvara from India
and the Taoist Queen of Heaven
switched places maybe
to make you *you*, Mother Kuan.

Footnote to Vietnam War

"It says here," said the student,
  settling her *Guardian Weekly*, bag of Doritos,
  and bouffant pillows on the floor,
"that the girl in the famous photo
  is grown-up now, and she
  advertised to meet the pilot
  who dropped the napalm
  that hit her ville."
"Oh?" said the bodhisattva.

"It says here," said the student,
"that the woman from the famous shot
  offered to forgive
  the American pilot
  who dropped the bomb
  that disfigured her,
  should she ever meet him
  in person."
"Yes?" said the bodhisattva.

"It says here," said the student,
"that a middle-aged man came forward
  and identified himself
  as the former pilot
  who dropped the napalm canister
  that incinerated her ville.
  It says here
  he's now a preacher."
"It's possible," said the bodhisattva.

"The woman with the reconstructed skin
  embraced the pilot-turned-preacher
  in an 'emotional meeting,' it says here,"
  over a reprint of the famous photo:
  seven sauntering soldiers,
  two glancing back
  at the ville alit,
  two gazing pensively at the roadway,
  none seeming to register
  the five children
  racing just ahead.
"Then the forgiven preacher
  put his story on the Internet."
"Hmm," said the bodhisattva.

"But then, it says here," reported the student,
  abandoning a Dorito in mid-munch,
"that the preacher and confessed napalmist
  turned out to have been
  nowhere near that burning ville
  and the girl in the famous photo.
  He wasn't guilty,
  after all," said the student.
"In a sense,"
  said the bodhisattva.

"Of course, he was lying,"
  granted the student,
  looking back at the sleepwalking soldiers:
  two darting glances
  at the smoke from the ville alit
  and one soldier on the edge

just trying
to light his cigarette.
"He wasn't responsible," said the student.
"In a manner of speaking,"
said the bodhisattva.

"I wonder," said the student,
rearranging her pillows restlessly,
"if this woman is expected to forgive him
for jerking her emotions around again,
as he—or someone—jerked her, her
relatives, her body, before?"
"Compassion is
unexpected,"
hazarded the bodhisattva.

"You won't believe this," said the student,
after scribbling for a few moments
in her journal on the floor.
"I must be so exhausted
from all the studying you give me
and so mixed up
by this news item
that I accidentally
wrote *balm*
instead of *bomb*."
"Some slip,"
said the bodhisattva.

The Thirty-Three Sites of Kannon
for Joe Chadwick

It might be a bare room
in a Palolo temple, with folded chairs
stacked against the wall,

but don't panic;
you can still bestride
the old country.

Take sand from the sites
in white packets
with black characters.

Lay out the packets,
walk the rows,
the thirty-three picturings of Kannon.

At each station light incense
or light a candle,
leave flowers.

Pace out the thirty-three sites
where a bodhisattva's breath
entered your life:

when Clifford gave Joe,
wheelchaired by AIDS,
a silent back rub;

when Joe, stilled, gaunt,
gave us a reading
of a Shakespeare sonnet:

"In me thou seest the glowing of such fire
that on the ashes of his youth doth lie . . .
consumed with that which it was nourished by";

when M. gave a toy dog
for Joe and Clifford's home altar,
"because I know you wanted a dog";

when V. gave her colorful belt,
"for someone with a priest's power,"
and B. gave him her Snoopy, Joe Cool;

when O. gave drives to visit Joe,
A. gave a tape of Sweet Honey in the Rock,
R. gave his tears;

when Clifford gave us,
in furious sunset,
the scattering of Joe's ashes:

brown with white flecks,
bone ground in the press, the fire,
like shell ground by tumble, by water—

beach sand
with wooden scoop,
abandoned on the beach;

when Clifford gave us that body
and let us dip ash,
a freed sheen of gold.

Then put your past in packets,
in white squares,
with black characters.

At each station drift incense,
light a candle,
leave.

Though it's a bare room,
here are the sand,
the sites,

the sights,
the sound,
the whole country.

Mr. Alzheimer's
for Alan MacGregor

    The last time I talked to MacGregor
    before his family recalled him,
    age forty-two, to a Care Home near them,
    he was eating his lunch
    from a brown bag
    packed by friends.
    He'd eat a bite of sandwich,
    then forget the rest,
    before recalled
    by a paper bag
    to pleasures
    remaining.
    He did
    bite into the apple:
    "I have remembers
    of picking apples
    snowbound."
    Maybe he recalled
    picking wine saps for his grandfather
    in Wisconsin sunlight.
    Maybe he recalled
    other people's poems:
    "After Apple-Picking,"
    "Snowbound."
    Maybe his brain stored all poems
    in the same secret groove,
    so that pulling one aqua strand

from his grandmother's sewing box
brought all spools,
tangled,
into a last remaining
gift poem.

His poem
recalled me
to the fact that this
bodhisattva man,
though bounded by the snow
of slow dying,
gave Gala, Alan, McIntosh, MacGregor,
all tumbled,
as if it were
the first time.

Holding On to a Bodhisattva

How did he learn to ferry us,
    remoras gripping
        his dorsal fin?
He must have
    caught the knack
        when yanked from his pool,
holding to forty friends
    long-lined
        by AIDS.
Then, dangling in air,
    gasping
        (before miraculously dropped
back to his depths,
    alone),
        he figured out even then
to let his clear scales scatter
    the breaking light
        into blues, mauves:
dazzling,
    dappled,
        lapping.

How Kuan Yin Loves

Does she give?
Does she accept?

Does she give tied red threads?
Does she accept tied red threads?

Does she give "the beauty of scarification"?
Does she accept "the beauty of scarification"?

Does she give down-home fried green tomatoes?
Does she accept down-home fried green tomatoes?

Does she bestow the yellow rings of Saturn?
Can she bear the yellow rings of Saturn?

Does she do his typing? a woman's typing? the typing for the whole group?
Does she accept an orange and purple gift scarf? Does she walk around in it?

Does she listen?
Does she tell all? Does she not tell all? Can she stand on one foot, for many hours?

Can she watch the stomach tube inserted through a nose?
Can she watch them cry?

Can she flow toward a bigger river? Can she hear both ocean and the thin trickle, back in the hills?
Can she accept their tributaries, without overflowing her banks?

Kuan Yin Hears Cries

Someone is crying.
No one is here.
Next to the impassive typist in tweeds
the blinking eye in the water cooler
is crying.
Three white mushrooms are crying,
though no one has kicked them over.
The deportees
are certainly not crying,
say the censored holes in the newsprint
whose tatters
are crying. The month of May
is crying. A sudden ice cream truck,
sticky with the past,
is crying its wares.
All the fathers in the world
are crying. China cups
which used to belong to someone
cry in the cupboard
against slippery saucers.
The evacuees are visibly crying
though sound transmission
has been broken.
The cut-back limbs of the ear pod tree
let down congealed tears
and cannot wipe them away.
The Marilyn Monroe look-alike
who waited in the hot sun to audition

is trying to cry.
The teddy bears left to witness in closed garages
are crying into fume-imbued plush.
The music leaking out of a Walkman
is causing to cry
as if it were the damped down jollying
inside a taxiing airplane.
The new round of departures is crying.
The new round of courtships is crying.
The lost vowels of a holy name are crying.
The stags whose horns have pushed up in velvet
are crying from shame at their beauty.
Kuan Yin's body on its bed
is hot with tears.

Buddha-Bodies

    Cushioned on running shoes
    (briefly halted)
    and weighted by amulets
    (cameras whose pig snouts
    ward off all chance
    of failure to see),
    two visitors
    swivel their necks to inspect
    thousand-armed Kuan Yin.
    They take note of
    those hands:
    some patting
    some strumming
    some fanning
    some fluffing
    some dandling
    some crumbling headlands
        back into foam
    some smudging blueberry skins
    some letting go
    some trailing through lily ponds
    some, with bitten nails,
        picking ticks
        from two thousand scalps
    some practicing *kung fu* chops
        on boardroom tables,
        coffee cups clattering
    some plaiting hair

some planting wrinkled radish seeds,
    each one separate
some stroking wispy beards of dragons
some holding smoke
some typing directories of the sad
    into the computer:
    six million K
some tossing crack seed in the parade
some sweating
some dangling, uncertain
some winding up a buzzing-bee toy for a toddler
    twenty times in a row
some guiding levers for the desperate at slot machines
some throwing out the worm-eaten radish crop
some unplaiting
some conjuring silver molecules
    on photographic paper
    into the glossy shadow play
    of Buddha-bodies.

Photograph Sites

Page 23	Chinese Cultural Plaza, Honolulu
Page 24	Chinese Cultural Plaza, Honolulu
Page 29	Chinese Cultural Plaza, Honolulu
Page 30	Chinese Cultural Plaza, Honolulu
Page 33	Chinese Cultural Plaza, Honolulu
Page 37	Chinatown shop, downtown Honolulu
Page 40	Thiền Viên Chân Không Vietnamese Temple, 'Āina Haina
Page 45	Palolo Zen Center, Honolulu
Page 46	*Guanyin Bodhisattva*, painted wood, China, Northern Song Dynasty, ca. 1025. Honolulu Academy of Arts Purchase, 1927 (2400).
Page 51	Chinatown shop, downtown Honolulu
Page 52	Thiền Viên Chân Không Vietnamese Temple, 'Āina Haina
Page 54	Chinatown shop, downtown Honolulu
Page 58	Kuan Yin Temple on Vineyard Boulevard, Honolulu
Page 60	Closed case from Shingon Mission, Wailuku, Maui
Page 63	Open case from Shingon Mission, Wailuku, Maui
Page 64	Chinatown shop, downtown Honolulu
Page 69	Chinese Society Building, Hawai'i's Plantation Village, Waipahu. This statue is said to be from a Fort Street Mall temple, now closed.
Page 71	Kwanseum bosal (Kuan Yin bodhisattva), Mu-Ryang-Sa, Korean Buddhist Temple, Honolulu
Page 72	Wo Hing Museum, Lahaina, Maui

Page 74	Wo Hing Museum, Lahaina, Maui: close-up view of preceding site
Page 79	Thiền Viên Chân Không Vietnamese Temple, 'Āina Haina
Page 82	Palolo Kwannon Temple, Honolulu
Page 87	Chinatown shop, downtown Honolulu
Page 89	Palolo Zen Center, Honolulu
Page 90	Thiền Viên Chân Không Vietnamese Temple, 'Āina Haina
Page 94	Chinatown shop, downtown Honolulu
Page 101	Korean Kwanseums from John Young Museum, University of Hawai'i at Mānoa
Page 102	Chinatown shop, downtown Honolulu
Page 106	Palolo Kwannon Temple, Honolulu
Page 111	Mural of Kwan Yin at Miramar Hotel, Kūhiō Avenue, Honolulu
Page 117	Raigō Kannon, carved and gilded wood, Japan, Kamakura Period (1185–1393). Honolulu Academy of Arts Purchase, in memory of Edie Boas, 1992 (7142.1).
Page 118	Scrimshaw by artist Paul Sheldon, Honolulu
Page 123	Reverend Eshin (Irene) Matsumoto, Palolo Kwannon Temple, Honolulu
Page 124	Palolo Kwannon Temple, Honolulu: Joe Singer and Kathy Phillips with granite Kwannon
Page 135	Bishop Museum, Honolulu. The two figures accompanying Kuan Yin are the Dragon Princess and Sudhana.
Page 139	Thiền Viên Chân Không Vietnamese Temple, 'Āina Haina
Page 140	Hawai'i Chinese Buddhist Society, Nu'uanu, Honolulu
Page 146	Main altar at Mu-Ryang-Sa, Korean Buddhist Temple, Honolulu: Shakyamuni Buddha is in the center. To his right sits Maitreya, a Buddha of the future. To his left sits Kwanseum (Kuan Yin).
Page 148	Jewelry store, Lahaina, Maui
Page 152	Siam Imports, Honolulu

Acknowledgments

"It's Natural." *La'ila'i: Anthology of the Women's Center Reading Series.* Ed. T. M. Lafferty. Vol. 1. Honolulu: Hawai'i Literary Arts Council, 1994. 36.

"Kuan Yin, Inventor," "Speaking to Kuan Yin." *Sister Stew: Fiction and Poetry by Women.* Ed. Juliet S. Kono and Cathy Song. Honolulu: Bamboo Ridge Press, 1991. 318–21.

"Ryozen's White-Robed Kannon," "Kannon Submits to Freedom in the Tea Ceremony," "This Isn't a Picture I'm Holding." *Bamboo Ridge: The Hawai'i Writers' Quarterly* 44 (Fall 1989): 27–31.

"Kuan Yin Faces Charges," "Lesson in Ink." *Chaminade Literary Review* 2.2 (Spring 1989): 79–81.

"Kuan Yin Hears Cries." *Chaminade Literary Review* 1 (Fall 1987): 1–2.

"Kuan Yin Is Mobbed by Reporters at Honolulu International Airport," "Valley of the Temples, O'ahu" "Wake," "Kuan Yin Turns Her Photo Album to a Certain Point," "Crack Seed," and "Kuan Yin Mingles with the Ghosts, Now on Guided Tour, of the Slave Population Which Constructed the Great Wall of China." *Bamboo Ridge: The Hawai'i Writers' Quarterly* 25 (Winter 1985): 9–15. The last three of these poems reappeared in *The Best of Bamboo Ridge* 31–32 (1986): 74–76. "Kuan Yin Mingles with the Ghosts" was reprinted in *Blind Donkey* 11 (July 1989): 13 (published by Diamond Sangha, a Zen Buddhist society, in Honolulu).

About the Author and Photographer

Kathy J. Phillips received a Ph.D. in comparative literature from Brown University. She is a professor of English at the University of Hawai'i, where she received an Excellence in Teaching Award in 1990. The more recent of her two books of literary criticism is *Virginia Woolf against Empire*. She has also published some twenty articles in such journals as *College English, Twentieth Century Literature,* and *Journal of Modern Literature*.

Joseph Singer is a photographer, artist, and writer with degrees in chemical engineering and chemistry from the University of Pittsburgh. After 1980 he turned his attention to sculpture, printmaking, and photography, using themes from Hawaiian culture, religion, and mythology, as well as from his own cultural roots. He has exhibited in many shows and has also worked on special commissioned pieces. He has been photographer and photographic resource for the University of Hawai'i anthropology department. He co-authored with Jan Becket *Pana O'ahu: Sacred Stones, Sacred Land*.

Phillips and Singer /
This Isn't a Picture I'm Holding: Kuan Yin

Produced by Wilsted & Taylor Publishing Services
  Interior designed by Tag Savage,
  with text and display type in Scala
  Copyediting by Rachel Bernstein

Cover Design by Santos Barbasa Jr.

Printing and binding by Versa Press, Inc.

Printed on 60 lb. Finch Opaque, 426 ppi